THE INNOVATOR INSIDE'S GUIDE TO SUCCESS

*A handbook for everyone to identify
and successfully implement innovation
from within an organization*

By J. Blundell

CONTENTS

INTRODUCTION

For a significant part of the last two decades I have been identifying, developing, and implementing innovation in organizations, both large and small, and within a variety of different industries, such as Media, Software, Biotechnology, and Education. From my experience, I have learned that you do not have to be in a senior position such as the CEO, C-Suite Executive, or a Manager to be a successful innovator in your organization. Anyone can innovate in the workplace. This book is intended to be a practical guide for innovators at any level of an organization, providing a path for discovering new ideas, implementing improvements, and making changes. The guide helps you to identify innovations and describes approaches and methods to value them, develop them, and to make them happen.

My primary desire is to share what I have learned from my real-world experiences in identifying, designing, and implementing new tools and process from within corporate and not-for-profit organizations. I hope that by sharing my knowledge and providing quick and simple methods for identifying, developing, and implementing innovations in the workplace, I will motivate you to develop your own ideas. It is enormously rewarding to see an idea grow into a product, process, or service and to see the benefits take effect. I want everyone to have the opportunity to experience that feeling. In addition to personal satisfaction, there are also many significant benefits in demonstrating yourself to be an employee that brings value to an organization through innovation and the ability to successfully implement change. Being an innovator will significantly differentiate you from your co-workers, who may all have similar educational and career histories. As well, it provides a path for individuals with a non-traditional background to fully realize their potential when that value may not be otherwise identified within the day to day work environment, allowing everyone to contribute in significant ways to the organizations they work for and experience a rich and fulfilling career.

Contained in this guide are methods and processes for identifying and defining potential innovations that exist within your organization; it provides guidance on how to get support from others and practical steps on how to manage the implementation process. I have successfully used these same techniques many times to implement a wide variety of innovations. Some examples of these are: new software technologies, organization-wide processes such as Enterprise Risk Management programs, revolutionizing old bureaucratic policies to strip away waste, building entire new departments to leverage cutting edge technologies and ideas, revealing paradigm shattering information, by improving communications within the organization, and driving strategic decision making by the Board and Senior Leadership by improving their understanding of an organization, along with many smaller department and office level changes to improve daily productivity. These can be some of the most impactful changes for creating a fulfilling work environment and increasing employee satisfaction.

Most importantly the techniques I describe are simple, easy to follow and have been refined to include the many lessons I have learned along the way – hopefully this speeds your journey along, and I sincerely hope that you can create improvements upon this book from your own experiences.

Finally, I would recommend that if there is a section that you find particularly interesting then go and read it in depth as you are likely to succeed most when you are working on innovations that focus on the things you most enjoy doing. The purpose of this book is as a practical lay guide for as many people as possible. It is my firm belief that every person working in a job has the potential to add additional value to their organization regardless of position, education, or background. You do not need an MBA to understand the basics of how an organization works, and you do not need a Ph.D. in mathematics in order to make use of the mathematics used in everyday work settings.

You can make a difference!

HOW TO IDENTIFY
INNOVATIONS

In this section, you will work through various tools and how to approach the initial identification of potential innovation opportunities that exist within your organization. It is important to recognize that not all innovations are necessarily changes you ought to make; some may be of greater importance to your organization and some less so. Some may be more important to you or to other individuals than they are to the organization as a whole. Because of the varying importance of any changes, the identification process must be made in a way that allows the comparison of all the different changes against some benchmark. The approach described in this section provides a framework to operate within, when using the various tools to identify innovations. I call this the "Value Approach to Innovation." The Value Approach to Innovation is straightforward and hinges around a single axiom. The reason for this axiom is to provide a firm basis upon which to develop ideas, assess outcomes, and be able to produce sound arguments. This section also details where to find and look for tools and ideas to use in identifying and implementing innovations, in addition to the ones you may already have acquired through your own experience, education, and training.

Innovation can, and should, build upon itself. As you work to develop innovations for your organization you will develop new skills and be exposed to new ideas, which can be used to generate further improvements, and tools to the existing processes and refine and improve on prior innovations.

VALUE APPROACH TO IDENTIFYING INNOVATIONS

The simplicity in use of the Value Approach to Innovation is its basis on just one single working axiom, which is that any innovation should "maximize resource value." Any focus of innovation should be upon maximizing the value of the resources available to the organization. In doing this to each individual innovation the following question shoudl be posed '... *in the long-term is this the best use of this resource?*'

Asking this one simple question is the foundation for building a complete picture of the value of each innovation. Because *value* is a subjective term, as is the *best use*, the *value* and *best use* will vary depending on the nature of any changes being considered and must be determined by the organization. Organizations determine the value and best use of any resources either explicitly by having a formal mission statement, declaration of values, and strategic goals, or less obviously, through the choices that senior leadership and the board make and the implicit values of those decisions. Most large and many small organizations have a defined mission statement, along with goals and values often published on their web pages, in training, investor or public communications materials. When these exist they should be used to determine the value of the change and if resources should be used.

To use the mission statement, or other clearly identified set of values that the organization holds, take the value question above *...in the long-term is this the best use of this resource?* using this question requires four steps:

> *...in the long-term ...is this... the best use of this resource to ... insert mission or value here?*

Step 1 - Determine what *is this*

The first change question is to specify what the *is this* really means by changing it to detail the innovation being considered. The *is this* will be the expected outcome of any innovation; this could be the details of what will change, but most likely is the expected outcome. What is the expected change that will occur or what objective will be achieved, either directly or indirectly, by implementing the innovation? The *is this* is not the activity but the outcome. It is not the process of building a web site, but the customer satisfaction from the ease of access to information.

Step 2 - Identify the resources involved

When considering what has to happen in order to implement your innovation, consider the five W's: Who, What, Where, When and Why these will help identify the resources you would need, what equipment or consultants, what time of your own and of others and would there be any need for new space. These are the resources that would be consumed that could be providing other value to the organization.

Step 3 - Set the organization's benchmarks

The second change is to add the organization *values* to the question.

Sometimes there are multiple values that the organization holds, which may hold equal importance. Just as when there is one mission or item you need to evaluate the innovation against, you follow the same process, dropping the organization's mission, values, or goals into the value question and considering if the change is valuable. Once this process is completed, and an answer found for every value, mission, or goal, the answers must be considered as a group. Any changes that have an answer to the value questions that indicate a potentially negative impact should be thrown out. Changes where all the answers to the value questions are either neutral or positive can be considered as potential candidates for implementation.

Step 4 - Answer the question

When reviewing the question as it has been adapted, would a reasonable person answer yes, no or it makes no difference?

The following example is given to show you how to transform mission statements and values into a decision making framework using the value questions.

For Example:

You have just started working in the new student inquiries department for a university. You were attracted to the job in part because of the organization's mission to *educate students to the highest standards.* Your role, amongst many tasks, also involves responding to emails from potential new students, by creating a record, entering the details and responding. After six months you have found that you get enquires about many different things, but 80% of them are for two or three recurring questions. You start to believe that adding these questions to the main web site would help reduce the volume of inquiries and give you more time for the unusual questions. After consulting your colleagues and making some discrete inquiries, you learn how the website gets updated. Adding the questions to the web site is not very difficult but does require approvals, having the Web team add a new section to the enquires pages, and having communications create the text.

So following through the four steps:

Step 1 - Determine what *is this*

Step 2 - Identify the resources involved

Step 3 - Set the organization's benchmarks

Step 4 - Answer the question

For each step go back to the example and review the scenario thinking about it for each step in answering the question.

Step 1 - Determine what *is this*

In this example, we need to determine what is the expected impact of the *is this*. Your expected impact is that you will have more time to help the unusual inquiries and the most common inquiries will be answered almost immediately as they will be publicly available:

This results in:

> *Step 1 = providing faster answers and more help to potential new customers*

Step 2 - Identify the resources involved

At the end of the example, you have identified what resources are needed, in addition to your own time. Adding the questions to the web site is not very difficult but does require approvals. Having the Web team add a new section to the enquires pages, and for communications to create the text.

This results in:

> *Step 2 = web team and communications time*

Step 3 - Set the organizations benchmarks

Early in the example, you mention that part of the initial attraction to the job was the organization's mission statement to *educate students to the highest standards*. Let's for simplicity, assume this is the only value the organization currently has.

This results in:

Step 3 = educate students to the highest standards

Step 4 - Answer the question

To answer the question, we need to put all the pieces from the last three steps back together, so:

'...*in the long-term is **providing faster answers and more help to potential new students** the best use of the **web team and communications time**, for the purpose of **educating students to the highest standards**'?*"

Thinking through the question you realize that some of those enquires will become students. Providing better information will help those potential students make better decisions about what choices they should make when enrolling as a student, ultimately positioning to be able to focus on learning, rather than dealing with administrative and academic changes which would distract and impede their learning experience. So, the change should, to a small extent at least, help to increase the educational standard for those students.

This results in:

Step 4 = Based on that analysis, this is a change worth investigating further!

It is important to remember that this process is a filter to remove changes that are not in the best interest of the organization by determining if the change has value to the organization as a whole. It does not provide an absolute determination of if an innovation is viable, or if it should be pursued to completion. Approaching innovation, change, and other improvements from a value perspective will ensure your changes are aligned to the rest of the organization and can be built upon by yourself and others without significant revisions.

In some cases organizations can have multiple values, for example, Patagonia's "Build the best product, cause no unnecessary harm, use business to inspire and implement solutions to the environmental crisis." has three separate components to its mission statement

The critical point here is that the determination of *value* comes from advancing that mission, conforms to the values of the organization and is supporting the current strategy. As mentioned earlier, the innovation value statement should be rephrased to incorporate the mission or any other relevant goal or value, and in doing so it becomes. *In the long-term is this the best use of this resource to [insert mission statement]?* In the case of Patagonia, there are several facets to the mission statement. Each one of these would be weighted equally and decisions made against three sets of scales, the preferable option is the one that supports each one. Even if an innovation supports one facet of the mission statement extraordinarily well it must not be in conflict with the others.

Another use of the value approach to innovation

The value approach to innovation can also be used for other purposes. For example, it can be beneficial during meetings that become trapped in a circular argument, or on some specific idea or technical and historical facts to step back and ask yourself about the discussion, *In the long-term is this [whatever is being discussed] the best use of this resource [what the meeting was originally about]?* By thinking about this it provides context to determin if you should continue the discussion, and if not a logical reason for asking the group to shift back. This method can be a way of breaking a cycle of analysis or argument that has deviated significantly from the original purpose or is no longer relevant to the decisions that need to be made. Doing this will help to avoid roadblocks where there may be no right answer because the solution is not present in the original conversation and perhaps a more comprehensive discussion needs to take place that can identify a third way or a longer-term solution. This is not always an easy thing to do, and there may be meetings where you do not feel you can make this choice. Perhaps it's not your meeting, or you are a junior member of the discussion and don't know if you have all of the relevant information to be able to determine if it is a valuable use of people's time.

One final note on the Value approach to Identifying Innovation; this method requires that the mission statement of an organization genuinely represent the mission and values of the organization, if it does not then your innovation may not receive support, or if implemented may be less successful than anticipated. If early on you start to find unexpected arguments against any innovations, or you see changes taking place that seems out of line with the organization's mission statement, you may want to examine the actions of the organization against the mission statement. If you find they are not consistent with the mission statement you should create an adapted version, for yourself, which reflects the organization's actual mission as carried out by the members of the organization and supported by senior leadership.

The most prevalent adaptation to the mission statement you are likely to come across is for publicly traded organizations. These organizations may have mission statements that fail to represent that there is significant pressure to achieve positive short-term financial results, that comes from the owners of the business (the shareholders) expectations of share value growth or returns on their capital. In this case, you can simply add to the analysis a value that reflects this, such as the need that any innovation is either neutral on revenue growth, or in a more demanding environment that it will positively impact profits within no more than one operating cycle. There may be exceptions to this rule of thumb such as where a well-communicated plan to implement an innovation is enacted over a longer period of time, even when there are expected short-term impacts on revenue or profits. This is dependent on the communications providing shareholders with the confidence that it will be successful and offer higher future returns. However, achieving this would be a significant undertaking and would involve senior leadership and probably board member involvement.

Remember, the value approach to innovation is used to compare competing priorities by examining their demand on resources. As mentioned above, the entire purpose of the process is to help ensure any changes engaged in are of real value to the organization and making the best use of the limited resources available. To do this, there must be a way to measure value, creating a scale against which to balance decisions. The value method uses the mission statement or other stated values and goals of an organization to set this scale and create a way to measure value. This is to focus on the value to the organization and making sure decisions and changes are all in support of achieving its overall mission, and synchronize each member of the organization to work together.

Before you can make use of the value method you will have to have some ideas to test using it. The next section details some approaches and tools to help do this.

TOOLS AND APPROACHES FOR IDENTIFYING INNOVATION

Y ou may already have one or more ideas for changes and improvements within your organization. If so, this section will provide you with tools and approaches to identify innovation and help you to identify additional changes. It will help you to clarify those thoughts on where something needs to change, when you're not sure, yet, what exactly the changes need to be. In this section, you will learn more about how to identify those areas of the organization that may offer significant potential for innovation and improvement and determine the specific details of what that change should be. This section begins with the overall approach that should be taken in order to successfully identify innovations, along with tools to help identify the primary areas of the organization that offer the most significant opportunities for innovating.

Understanding the Organization & Environment

Your initial approach to implementing any innovations in an

organization should begin with learning. Taking the time to thoroughly understand how and why the current systems and processes exist the way they are. Understanding is critical. Regardless of if you have worked somewhere for twenty years or two months, it is imperative that you confirm carefully that you fully understand what is happening. Ideally, physically draw out either on paper or using basic shapes in a spreadsheet or word processor, all the connections or interrelationships of:

People – *every person who is involved, what they do*

Technology – *each system used and why it is used that way*

Processes – *how and where do things interconnect and why*

The smoothest path to follow when learning is through examining your daily routine. Look at the tasks you are performing and how you are interacting with the rest of the organization. Be inquisitive and curious about what the people and things you work with are doing. Perform mental exercises by spending time thinking about what you do, how it relates to the rest of the organization and consider this within the context of *why* as a great starting point for understanding how all of the things taking place are related to keep the organization running.

Some of the processes you come across may well be hard to understand, if not impossible, without outside assistance, so don't be afraid to ask. Most people enjoy talking about what they do and will happily help you understand. It may mean waiting until they have time though. For instance, I would not expect the accountants to be particularly chatty at the end of the financial year, as they are trying to close the books. You may find it useful, depending on the people and organization, to find out more by taking lunch with others or offering to buy them a tea or coffee.

In the case where a well-established event takes place that may seem, to the outside observer, either overly complicated, counter-intuitive or just plain crazy, chances are it is more likely than not the only way it can be done (or perhaps used to be) due to some other process, or technology. Assume your coworkers are intelligent. If they could do it differently, they probably would. More likely than not, time and other commitments mean that just getting it done is a challenge, let alone reviewing the whole process and seeing if it could be changed. Keep in mind also that these types of tasks are precisely the areas that may benefit the most from examination and offer opportunities for adding value, freeing up resources for more critical and valuable tasks.

From a practical point of view, there are endless ways to go about mapping and understanding processes and systems. I would recommend taking one small piece at a time, starting with the things you do, then cycle through areas in which you already have visibility. So, for instance, it might be a process that sits entirely within your own domain, such as the way new data is handled before it is entered into a system. Then follow that information where it goes, why and what it is for. By being guided by the flow of activity from well-understood processes such a the ones you perform yourself, and that impact you directly, you will begin to learn and understand more processes and events further afield, and eventually throughout the organization. This process has the additional benefit that it will help to identify other areas of the organization that may directly affect you and allow you to better plan. Beginning with yourself and your own actions will help you understand your own work in ways you may not have considered and will become a foundation for understanding.

As you build your understanding of the organization, and the mapping of processes and workflows becomes more complex, you will need to find ways to help keep a clear picture of what is happening, where and with who. There are many different ways to help document and remember the relationships of various activities and processes; the most commonly used are flow diagrams. There are specific standards for the use of shapes and designing flow diagrams that you can research and use if you will be sharing this with others whom you know will use those standards. If you are not going to use your mapping with others or any groups that will not need the standards then simply make it up as you go along, be consistent in what shapes and colors you choose for different meanings. You don't have to use flow diagrams or special software. Whatever you do, try to keep it simple and remember the point is to help build understanding. You're not going to be graded on it, if coloring in helps, then go ahead. If detail drawings drive you nuts and you work best with lists then, by all means, use written lists. Just make sure you can quickly change it as you learn more and that it has all of the steps, people and technology. I use whatever seems to make the most sense to me at the time, a big cardboard box covered in post-it notes, whiteboards I like for getting the basic ideas down, and then Word, PowerPoint, and Excel are all easy to use and store.

I am not suggesting you try to document every detail and every process, person and technology, although I have to admit it always seems tempting to try. Instead, this is a chance to develop a broad understanding of interconnections and flows of work and information within the organization and how it communicates in order to function. Later this knowledge will be useful for identifying areas of value, and in helping to implement any changes. It will also be useful in identifying areas that are not impacted in any way and do not need to be detailed. It is at this point when you have identified an innovation to be implemented that you will need to flesh out your broad, high-level understanding with specific details. If there is an area you are already interested in, you may want to begin gathering details while you continue to build your high-level understanding. For instance, once you have mapped some process or activity, follow it as it actually occurs. This may mean waiting for a year or more if it's related to something that only happens rarely. Be patient, be flexible so that as your information changes, you can change your mind. Make sure what you think is happening is a complete picture of everything that happens.

If you don't understand, on a broad level at least, everything that is happening when you come to attempt to make changes you may find you are trying to implement a change that may be fantastic, but is an excellent solution for a problem or issue your organization does not have. In some cases, you may not have a complete innovation or one that only partially fits the needs of the organization. If you are unaware of the incomplete or unsuitable aspects of a change you could end up forcing through an innovation through that does not truly resolve inefficiency. Such forced changes may end up introducing more issues, removing any benefits and potentially exacerbating a situation and reduce the value of what should have been a success. In essence you will have the square solution for a round problem.

Identifying Innovation Opportunities

There are a few useful common identifiers that can help you determine opportunities for innovation. I have attempted to group these below and give a very high-level summary of what you might expect to see or be experiencing when these identifiers are around. It is important that you do not underestimate your own ability to identify opportunities for innovation which may not fall into any of the categories below. They could be based on your instincts and intuition, trust yourself and look further into it.

Noise – This is probably the most significant clue; people are very good at identifying processes that are outside their normal expectations. Complaints can give you a hint that there is something not working particularly well and help you to focus in on whatever it is. The complaints may also help identify a solution. It could be likely that the complaints are coming from individuals that are experiencing a similar event elsewhere, but is working better. Somewhere you may find some similar process being done, or something similar at least is happening in a different and possibly more effective way. Any time you find yourself repeatedly sighing as you start a process you have found something worth reviewing.

Age – Has anything changed for a specific function or task in many years? If not, this is an area worth review. Things change all the time, not only the technology but also the reasons, desires, and requirements of users. You may discover an opportunity to update a process that has been overlooked and could provide additional value to the organization. On the other side, how many technologies are clustered in one area or how many times has something been changed recently? Constant newness can also be a signifier of fixes for a process or task that needs a more in-depth review.

Sediment – How many different people and departments are involved, how many processes or forms or sites do you have to go through to get something done? If there are many people, sites, processes and anything else involved, and especially if they seem to weave through various and sometimes surprising, areas it could be evidence of processes that have built up one at a time becoming layered on top of one another causing overlapping areas and inefficiencies. These slow overlapping situations can often be vast hoggers of people's time and effort. Because of the overlap, the complexity can also often be very high and depending on the organization's culture, can be difficult to change as it can mean a large number of individuals facing change and the anxiety that can produce.

Plate spinning – You can get used to the odd quirks of things, and they become part of the scenery. However, if you find that there are things that continuously require attention and energy to keep them moving and to prevent them being dropped, a little like trying to keep plates spinning on poles, then you most likely have an opportunity to make some improvements.

Another excellent way of spotting opportunities in your organization is by staying current in your field of work, and attending conferences both inside and outside of your industry. You may even find inspiration in hobbies or through attending classes and reading industry journals. Even talking to some of those sales calls, that perhaps you usually ignore, can help bring in new ideas for all sorts of areas. Also, don't just restrict yourself to one region or country; there is a whole planet of ideas to mine.

Another significant potential source of ideas for innovation is within the business world itself. Large corporations spend billions trying to gain competitive advantages. There is no reason not to look at those organizations and see if you can work out what it is they are doing, and see if there is something you can apply to your organization. In this regard, using the ideas from the corporate world can be useful. It may be harder to find out what some organizations do that others do not without some digging. Start with businesses you have heard of from other individuals or that are particularly successful. Begin with the mission statement and look at the materials being published for investors. Compare these across businesses that seem to be similar in their success and look for the things that link them together.

Narrowing Down the Innovation Choices

In order to value any improvements for the organization, as well as making it possible to implement, you will need to define the innovation. What are the exact changes needed, what are the expected outcomes (benefits) and what evidence do you have to expect this outcome?

Using the value approach to innovation you have already been able to focus attention on the innovations likely to have value to the organization. Chances are there are several different options available to you to follow up on. So in order to help determine which ones to proceed with you need to build a better picture of what is involved in each innovation. In the development and planning section, you will review in more detail the concept of balanced change, where three key factors are considered in depth in order to ensure the smooth implementation of any innovations. These three factors critical to balanced change are used to better understand what is likely to be involved in any change and how much work and preparation may be needed before you are in a position to begin. The three key factors for balanced change are Analytical, Sociological, and Technological. At this early stage of high-level review the types of things to consider for each of these three are:

Analytical = How easy is it to get data or understand what is happening? How much data and what type is involved? Do you truly understand the information; such as how it is collected to ensure you're decisions are based on complete information? How much time will it take to analyze the information? Are your assumptions for analysis correct?

Sociological = How comfortable is your organization with change? Are there areas or departments that are more open to change? Are there any areas where change is going to be very difficult? Who are the decision makers? What is the functional hierarchy of who needs to *Approve* changes? What do individuals in the organization respond well to? What level of understanding of technology does your organization have, is that evenly spread? How well does your organization communicate? How easy is it to disseminate or gather information?

Technological = What technologies are already in place? How easy are they to use, or adapt? Is access to technology spread through the organization? What are security and implementation policies? What new technologies exist that could be used? How many changes would need to take place, one server changed or every laptop? What are the constraints on technology use?

When looking at the various factors you should write down and assign a ranking for each question you think of or answer. There are an almost infinite number of different questions you might ask depending on the combination of the innovation you want to implement, the organization you are in, and the availability of technology. At this stage you are still comparing ideas to help determine what innovations to implement so you do not need to tackle every tiny detail, Do, however, look for potential pitfalls or issues, which this exercise is designed to help highlight. Using a simple scale from one to five with one being the lowest or easiest and five being the highest or hardest rank the answers to your questions for each of the three factors. To make the different innovations comparable, take the average for each of the three factors. The simple mean of the total ranking for each question in the factor and divided by the number of questions. This gives a rough guide to how hard or easy each innovation is by each factor: Analytical, Technological and Sociological. You may feel more comfortable with a particular area and so a higher score in that may not be of as great concern. For example, perhaps you are highly technologically savvy and understand the organization's technological structure exceptionally well so a high score here is not as important as a high score in an area you feel less confident with so you would rank the potential innovations differently. If you are equally confident, or nervous, about each of the three factors you might want to take the average of the group to see each innovation as one score, simply adding together each of the three scores and dividing by three.

The purpose of this process is to help identify which innovations are the most likely to succeed based on your strengths. An essential part of this is the opportunity to think more deeply about each of your innovation ideas, trying to identify all the constraints and barriers as well as benefits, in addition to those you have already. Think about what technological, sociological, and what analytical issues there are and what things you are unsure of. You should also consider sequencing. Does implementing one of the innovations remove constraints that might lower the scores for other innovations? Consider if they naturally follow an order for implementation.

In the next section, we will take the innovation you have chosen and begin to flesh out the details. If during this process you come across some issue that makes it unimplementable come back to this section and your original work and re-rank based on the new information you have for all the innovations and simply get started with the next one.

DEVELOPING AND PLANNING THE IMPLEMENTATION

Once you have decided on a particular innovation to implement a more detailed and comprehensive view of the innovation itself is required, along with the exact way in which the innovation will be implemented. Developing your innovation and the planning process go hand in hand. You can use the planning process to refine your ideas and to identify any details that you may not have already considered but that may prevent or require a serious rethink of what you want to do. This is the process necessary to make absolutely certain that any innovations and changes you take forward are possible and successful.

DETERMINING THE IMPLEMENTATION STRATEGY

I mplementing innovation will fall into two categories. This will determine the overall strategy to take for successfully implementing the project. Innovation is either evolutionary (transformative) or revolutionary (disruptive).

To determine which category of change your innovation falls into you will have to consider the innovation in contrast to the current state of the organization or the process. To do this you should think about several things.

Can you break down the implementation of the innovation without interfering with the current state?

Can the two operate together? Over time, do the functions and activities smoothly transition from one to the other?

Does the introduction of one require the complete removal of the other?

Hopefully, as you were thinking about those questions you noticed that the answers vary based on the time frame you are considering. For example, can you make small changes to the existing system over a long time or does it all need to happen quickly in a short space of time? What ever you consider to be long or short term alters the project from being evolutionary to revolutionary.

There are some common traits and combinations of attributes that can help determine what type of change you are looking at when regarding the expected impact of the change in its entirety:

Can this change stand alone and be completed with almost no effect on any formal or informal processes, activities, technologies, or impacting the current state? If you can answer 'yes,' treat as evolutionary. If 'no' then treat as revolutionary.

Do you need to make small changes to the current state that reasonably are unlikely to have any impact or even be noticed? If you can answer 'yes,' treat as evolutionary. If 'no' then treat as revolutionary

Will you have to run two or more current and original things concurrently before switching into the change? If you can answer 'yes,' treat as revolutionary. If 'no' then treat as evolutionary

In the end, will the results of the change be the immediate elimination of one or more current system, process or activity? If you can answer 'yes,' treat as revolutionary. If 'no' then treat as evolutionary

Can you stop part way through with no negative impacts on the ability of the system(s) involved to function? If you can answer 'yes,' treat as evolutionary. If 'no' then treat as revolutionary

The object here is to get an idea of how best to approach the innovation project. It's possible you have two contradictory answers to the above questions, in which case you will need to think carefully about the impacts of the innovation. As a rule of thumb if there is an answer that's revolutionary, then it will likely need to be treated as revolutionary when thinking about what type of planning is necessary and what to expect. This is in order to try and take the approach that will make the best use of the resources available to you. However at the end of the day, a well thought out and carefully planned strategy is the most crucial aspect. Everything else is maximizing value on the resources being used, but it will not necessarily determine the success or failure of any endeavor.

Strategy For Evolutionary (Transformative) Change

Think of evolutionary change as a journey, breaking down a larger innovation into either smaller innovations spread over time, or the entire project into smaller sections. In general, evolutionary change is less risky, more likely to be accepted, and in the event of some alterations to the environment you are operating in, it is more easily adapted to unexpected changes. The downsides are that it takes time to implement and to see the results of any innovations. In some cases the entire vision may become obsolete before it is complete, although when done well the intervening steps will have been useful and added value. As such it is vital to ensure that the value of the steps you are taking are in proportion to the return on the assets utilized. When planning for evolutionary changes consider the value and stages where you could stop to take advantage of future options to change the overall direction or stop altogether so that more valuable innovations can take place. If there is significant utilization of resources at the start of an evolutionary innovation, or a significant proportion of the total resources to be used occour in the early stages of implementation, then consider carefully whether this is really suitable to be implemented over a long period of time. You may decide that to be a viable project the innovation must be reconsidered as revolutionary and implemented in one fell swoop.

Like a journey, evolutionary change is about having several smaller plans for each stop on the way, each as a small discrete project in of itself with the feedback from the prior stops updated into it as you go along. Tasks will move in series one after another; some may be able to run consecutively. The plans for the later steps will not be as detailed, if containing much detailed at all, as they will need to be updated with additional information gathered during the first stages of an evolutionary change.

Strategy For Revolutionary (Disruptive) Change

Revolutionary change can be thought of as a leap forward. This is the most exciting way to do it, you will see immediate benefits, and it is going to be relatively fast-moving, and the organization will see the benefits within a short period of time which, depending on the scale of the innovation, could be significant. The downsides are that if you have made a miscalculation or something changes in between the development planning and execution there is a considerable risk that the whole innovation may fail, and the impact of failure could be substantial depending on how widespread the innovation is within the organization.

The overall strategy for a revolutionary change is to have a very complete and highly detailed plan. The most significant difference is that the plan is developed extensively in advance. Because the plan is prepared almost entirely in advance, any changes to the plan may require numerous updates which ripple throughout the planning documents. The best plans will have contingencies for extra time or alternative approaches for three types of issue:

1) For the areas of the plan where you expect there may be some

delays or issues that need resolving

2) In critical parts of the plan where an issue could create a significant impact

3) Anywhere you have activity outside of your direct control, and need additional time for following up and providing feedback

In addition to contingencies, the planning for a revolutionary change should also include an outline for crisis management. This outline should set out the basics of how to respond to a severe problem should it arrive during the implementation or development. The crisis management outline should detail who, either individuals or groups, should be contacted, how that contact should be made, and at what point during a crisis that contact should be initiated. The crisis management outline should also list the roles and responsibilities of team members or those involved in a project so the correct people within the team are engaged as early as possible. The crisis management outline should be kept as simple as possible so that it is a straightforward, easy to read document that can be used in as wide a variety of situations as possible. The objective is to bring in the key team members and key stakeholders under predefined conditions as a crisis emerges. The document should also list some of the resources that can be called upon in the event they are needed.

Managing the number of interactions between all the various parts of the plan is going to become much more difficult the larger the scale of any innovation and the more people involved. As the number of people working on a project increases the risk of information not moving accurately all the way through a process or in a timely manner, becomes ever greater. To avoid this situation, it is imperative to make sure that in larger plans, communication is included as a specific item in each part of the plan, and made as easy as possible.

DEVELOPING
THE PLAN

T he twelve steps below provide an overview of the planning process that would be followed for either the evolutionary or revolutionary innovations. The overall strategy driving the content, level of detail, and timing of the plans would vary depending on the type of innovation, but the basic steps remain the same. Planning is a dynamic activity and will be different for every innovation you choose to implement, so these high-level steps are provided to get you thinking about your overall plan and should be updated as you work through each step:

1. Gather and quantify data that helps to confirm that the innovation is adding value. You may need to ask others for help. For instance, if this innovation is going to reduce a manual process, then what is the scale, how many are there, or how much time is taken?

2. Identify the benefits specifically for others. What other information might be useful to stakeholders, such as senior leadership in building a case for funding if required, or users to help identify how it benefits them. Do the changes make their lives easier, will it save money that can be used for other things, and does it allow other things that they may want to take place or

become easier?

3. Develop precise models of existing processes, workflows, or designs to make sure that you fully understand how the innovation will impact the organization. You will use these to show the impact of the innovation on the organization and to individuals, you will need to be able to assuage any concerns, and the first step towards this is being confident in answering the question how will it impact me, or my work?

4. Create very basic mockups or drafts of what you hope the outcome will be. For instance, if you are adding a technical change, use a basic office tool, or even paper, to help show how the design will look and what features will be included. This can be used to get feedback from any others impacted or those that might use it and help identify additional value or avoid potential pitfalls before very much has been invested in design and development.

5. Identify the names of users and those directly impacted. This listing will be necessary to get buy-in and acceptance as well as determine whom you might need to be involved in the design, testing, and implementation?

6. Identify any parts of the business cycle that will be impacted are there certain times of year that individuals are unavailable or is there a logical time to make any changes that minimize the impact or maximizes the benefits.

7. Develop a detailed time frame, weekly at least, and project plan of when things will happen. What are the key points when something has to happen based on other fixed events?

8. Develop an implementation plan, which includes

testing, identifying corrections and making changes. How are you going to roll out the innovation, a small group at first or to everyone at once? How are you going to do testing? How do you make sure you find all the issues? How are you going to coordinate for timing with those that need to be involved? How do you get those needed involved? How can you make sure everyone feels some ownership and that they had their voices heard?

9. Review the timeline; look at what events might be rearranged to reduce the impact, what could be run concurrently, what are the hard stops? Is there a cut off point where you can decide to delay if there are too many issues or unexpected problems come up, what is the point of no return?

10. Develop a communications plan. What are the different constituents, and how do you best communicate with them, how often and in what way. Do you use email, meetings or something else?

11. Develop standard materials, templates to use for all communications and products such as training materials. Ensure that everything you present or create is at the same high quality you would expect from a high-quality organization you admire. This includes coloring and branding, ideally with your organization's standard colors and logos as appropriate.

12. Pick a name for your project and have fun with it. If you are able to bring a sense of excitement and positive energy with you, it will be infectious and help build momentum.

The plan is what you think you're going to do; it is not necessarily what will happen, and that's ok. A plan should be flexible and it will change as new information comes to light, as you work on gathering and compiling the information for the twelve steps. You are likely to find at least one thing that causes a change elsewhere. Changes like this are a good sign that you are getting close to a firm understanding of the components and precisely how things are operating.

The plan you develop is a map of how you expect to get from where you are now to where you want to be and is what will keep you oriented. Keep the plan as up to date as possible. If the project is expected to take more than a couple of months make sure to include regular updates in the planning process timeline to revisit the details and keep them up to date. If some event happens, the plan will help to keep you oriented and allow you to be flexible in adapting. Just like if you find a road closed, with an up-to-date map, you can quickly work out a new path to where you want to go.

DEVELOPMENT & IMPLEMENTATION TOOLS AND APPROACHES

I n this section, you are going to think about where to find tools to help develop innovation. In this guide, tools for innovation include not only traditional physical tools, software, and hardware, but also approaches, policies, and methods of organizing workflows and behaviors.

An excellent place to start finding tools is through research on the internet around areas of interest that relate to your regular work and looking for what's new and what might be interesting. Often new ideas may not be directly replicated in your organization, but look for the aspects of those ideas that might be useful to you.

The Balanced Change Approach

Attempting to keep this book as generally useful as possible, I am going to give an overview of the three most basic categories of tools: Analytical, Sociological and Technological. I will give an explanation of what type of tools are found in these categories, most common uses, benefits, and potential challenges. I have broken the tools and methods into these three categories because it is critical to give equal consideration and thought to what tools to use in each of these areas to implement innovation within your organization. The amount the tools are used during a project will vary on the nature of the project however when initially planning you should spend the same amount of time and energy selecting and verifying the correct tools are being used for each category.

The diagram below shows the three primary categories of tools and their interrelated nature. This triangle represents 'Balanced Change.' As mentioned before, each of these factors should be given equal weight when under consideration, even if one area may be more heavily utilized during a project. When selecting and thinking about the tools to be used in each category, it is imperative to consider its impact on the tools being used in the other two categories reviewing the following:

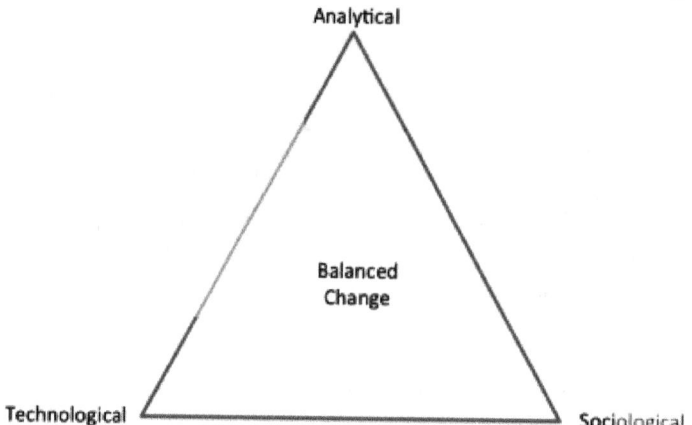

- **Analytical** - Analyzing the analytical techniques and approaches that can be used to understand the Sociological and Technological factors of any innovation.

- **Sociological** - Organizational environment in which any analysis will take place and technology will be deployed needs to be understood and documented to ensure the optimal tool sand approaches are used.

- **Technological** - Technology already in place and technology that may be available that can be leveraged for analysis and optimizing the sociological factors.

Innovation related changes will be needlessly complicated, more expensive, and risk failure if these three areas are not given equal consideration.

Analytical Tools and Approaches

Analyzing the sociological and technological aspects of your innovation requires that you use data and knowledge that is already available to you, as well as researching where and how you can learn more. For data, this begins with a fundamental analysis of what tools are used, what data is collected, how and where it is stored. It is vital that you understand the limitations of any data that you have including what it does and does not include. How the data is entered and collected will be valuable in that process.

Once you have gathered data together, you will need to use it to understand how the organization is likely to respond to change and to build a case for making change happen to begin with. To help with this, there are three sections below: Basic Statistical Techniques, Analytical Decision Making and Using Standards for Quantitative Analysis. These are simple outlines of the types of tools you can use. For a larger innovation, you may want to engage with financial analysts or other finance professionals to help build a stronger picture and understanding of the information. The contents of these three sections is designed to give you a starting point by providing a reminder on the language so that when looking for help from analysts, or others, you are able to speak to what you need.

As with all points in implementing an innovation, you should think carefully about your strengths and weaknesses, and what time you have to learn, to help in deciding when it is better to engage a partner or team member who has those skills. When thinking about team building, think about the balanced change approach and build a team with a broad range of skills that can cover the three primary factors of Analytical, Sociological, and

Technological.

Analytical Decision Making

In order to rank the innovation and build a strong case for implementing any changes, it is important to be able to quantify, compare, and contrast various activities. Being able to quantify aspects of any change and compare it to the current state is critical in making sound decisions. Most importantly, it helps to insulate decision making from personal biases and short-term impulses.

Quantitative = Numbers such as quantities of thing. For instance, you can quantify the number of tickets sold to an event by counting them.

Qualitative = the qualities of things. For example, the tickets are being sold to people in a particular zip code.

Quantitative analysis uses numbers such as sales information or income to try to make predictions or understand the likely results of certain events in a specific environment. Often assumptions are made based on qualitative features.

For Example: Looking back at past events, we see that individuals who brought tickets from a specific zip code spent more on concessions. Looking at this we might decide that they spend about $25 more per ticket. We check this assumption by looking at other information about the Zip code. For instance, the average household income is much higher, so it seems reasonable that they may have a higher disposable income. This is quantifying a qualitative aspect so that we can use it to model expected revenue; we feel good that this is a likely result as it is backed up by history and a reasonable explanation for why these individuals might spend more. Now we can build a model where we expect $25 additional revenue for every ticket sold to individuals from this zip code, adding this up we can project likely total revenue for an event.

The most significant risk in decision making with quantitative analysis is when it is applied in settings where significant judgments are required in quantifying qualitative aspect, deciding what to collect, how to group data, and in the interpretation of the results. The methodology used should always be consistent and made clear to users so they can raise questions and put the results in context.

There is also the risk that any analysis will not be as absolute as the mathematical results suggest. You may have a decent number the values underlying it which are questionable or based on quantification that is highly variable or requires significant judgment. This can lead to unexpected failures and questioning of the use of quantitative analysis. When you have results that appear more reliable than they are, it becomes an issue of setting expectations and detailing the impact of the analytical method, highlighting the risk of variability from the results of an analysis. If eight times out of ten quantitative analysis leads to sound decision-making, it is crucial to provide as broad a range of information as possible for decision-making. Doing so will help to avoid purely judgment based decisions which can be susceptible to "grou think" and ingrained prejudices. However, it requires careful thought and subjective reasoning, which can be improved with experience and knowledge in and around the area or environment that the innovation is going to impact.

An excellent example of the quantitative application analysis, where the results are very subjective, is in risk assessment. Here decisions must be made about various risks, and of the impact and likely occurrence of specific risk events. It is an excellent example of where judgment must often be used to quantify the risk and likelihood of an incident. Under ideal conditions, the individual closest to an event is the person who identifies and quantifies it; occasionally it may be a manager who is familiar with an event that subordinates processes. For the quantification, on occasion, the initial assessment can be based on empirical data, but often it is merely an informed individual making a judgment call, which will flow through all of the data and will influence the assessment of risk throughout an entire organization.

On face value, this may arguably seem pointless. If the judgment is not sound, what is the point of putting a number to something to quantify it? In the worst case it could be misleading, this is a reasonable objection, and it is why a firm understanding of the nature of the underlying data, how it was collected, and setting expectations with decision makers about what the process will produced is required from the beginning.

So why quantify if it is based on judgment anyway? Well, in the example of risk assessment, the process itself has value by making you and others think about risk and looking around them to identify them. If they are aware of the risk, it is already much less likely for it to have the same impact. Additionally, the data in and of itself is valuable, assuming that some normalizing of the data takes place, and quantifications are qualified as well. A third party can review and set the quantified levels to reduce noise in the data and to question rankings that are not what others might expect. Once completed this can be used to give a good overview of the risk status of an organization to senior leadership and the board, who would have little knowledge of the detailed level of risks in a medium to large organization. It provides leadership a way to prioritize fixes for risk areas that may require more resources in a way that can be easily communicated to management, and also help management to understand why one area might be given priority over another.

In this example, it is not just the results of the quantification and analysis that are valuable but also the process itself. In many cases where the outcome of quantitative analysis may seem only 85% reliable the value may be engaging in the process and thinking about the details and potential impacts.

Another important concept for analysis is the time value of money, how a dollar now is worth more than a dollar in a year's time. This concept also introduces the idea of opportunity cost too, where choosing to do one thing precludes the ability to do something else.

Broadly speaking the time value of money can be considered as two main ideas

1) **Inflation** - How things will cost more in the future and so you can expect to buy more with your dollar today than you can in the future. There are several different ways to try to measure inflation. The Bureau of Labor Statistics compiles one of the most famous with the Consumer Price Index (CPI) which is a historical measure of how a specific selection of goods have changed in price. There are also some central and commercial banks and international institutions such as the International Monetary Fund (IMF) that try to predict future inflation, which can be used for planning purposes.

2) **Return On Investment** - This is how much you might expect to receive in interest, dividends, or increased value from investing your dollars. For instance, in your savings account, perhaps your bank will pay interest to you. Generally the more risk of losing money, the higher the return you can expect for your dollar. This is the amount of money you lose by not investing your money.

The two combined give a projection of the expected value of your money: the return paid from the investment less inflation. So if the bank gives you 2% interest to save with them and inflation is 1.5%, your money will actually be 0.5% more valuable. You will be able to purchase 0.5% more than today (2%-1.5% = 0.5%) so the value has increased. However, if your bank only offers 1% interest then you will find your cash is actually able to buy 0.5% less, than it is today (1%-1.5% = -0.5%) as the value has decreased.

Organizations, and very likely yours too, have a minimum (hurdle) rate that they need to receive as a return on any investments. For many organizations this is the cost of capital. Often it is the Weighted Average Cost of Capital (WACC) expressed as a percentage, which is the expected cost of financing their activity. This cost is the amount of interest the organization must pay on money borrowed from the market, debt, or money invested by the owners (equity, for instance) shares for which the owners expect a return.

The reason organizations use the WACC to set the lower limit for the expected return on any investments is that any investment that returns less than this rate is yielding less than the organization is spending to get the cash to make the investments. For example if the WACC (the amount it costs to borrow money and get money from investors) is 4.5% and the cash that is borrowed as debt and investors is used on a project that can only expect to see returns of 3.5%, it is costing the organization 1% to do this project. Therfore the organization is losing money. Just like when comparing the inflation rate to return on cash it is important to remember that there is a time value component to cash. At a minimum inflation, and potentially it could affect organizational goals and limits. When you are looking at your innovation, in particular more substantial changes, you should be asking the question. "Is the cost to make the innovation, over the long term, worth the expected return?"

As a rough guide to thinking about the monetary value, identify the underlying activity that can be unitized, hours used, materials wasted, customers lost or gained into some discreet amount and then estimate how much it would cost. What is the average cost for that unit? Then compare the current cost of doing what you're doing to the expected cost of activity once the innovation is in place. The difference between those is the value $x. The total value to the organization, over the long term can be worked and compared to the cost of implementation by using the formula for the present value of a perpetual annuity. The formula = D/r where D equals the annual savings in $ and r equals the organizations minimum required rate of return on investment in %, or % expressed as a decimal. If the total present value of the innovation is greater than the implementation costs, then you have a good indication that this innovation would be a good use of the organization's resources.

Even though at first glance, Not for Profits (NFPs) may appear to have little in common with for-profits, it is possible to find common ground and to start to see how analytical techniques can be applied across both. To demonstrate the common ground consider that corporations' capital belongs to shareholders, in NFPs, like Higher Ed it is the donors, who for analytical purposes can be considered in the same way as shareholders. Shareholders give capital to businesses and if the company does not continue, then some portion of that capital is given back. Donors can endow capital that never belongs to the institution; it is given for the mission of the institution, along with any restrictions the donor may apply. If the institutions choose not to continue that mission, some portion of the funds may have to be returned to the original owners or their heirs. The institution is the steward of its funds. This similarity is even easier to visualize if the organization has a unitized endowment where the contributions have a given unit value, just as a share has a specific value unit value.

For the corporate world, the shareholders have given their capital with the expectation of some future monetary return. For donors, their capital has been given with the expectation of some future social return. The similarities continue in that the maximization of value is the key to maximizing the overall monetary or social return. Both measures of value contain plenty of intangible factors. Consider the price of a share where the monetary value is many times the claim on net assets, future growth, intellectual, managerial and other hard to quantify amounts which are being included in the price. So with Higher Ed, the intangible factors in social return such the benefits of a well-educated population, on economics, social justice, politics, health and the general happiness of society and individuals are included in the value.

Thinking along these lines helps to understand how to apply financial ratios and start to consider, that the cost of capital for a business and NFPs can be calculated in the same way. From this, it is easy to see how other financial tools and analytical methodologies from industry, such as Real vs. Nominal, Net Present Value (NPV), Return On Investments (ROI), Opportunity costs and other common analytical methods can be applied directly and usefully to not-for-profits as well as for-profits. Including more complicated financial tools, for example in corporations, it is not uncommon to use the Black-Sholes option pricing formula to get a better estimate of a large project that may be constructed in multiple phases by building in the cost of the 'option' to stop or develop further. By getting into the habit of determining simple ratios such as returns on investments, and slowly applying more complicated techniques, better-informed decisions can be made maximizing value. Everyone has the ability to understand both the more common analytical methods, and use these as a foundation to learn other more complex ones. Please do not be put off by any unfamiliar terminology. It can seem like the banking and finance world has a language of its own, but it is mostly just a lot of old world words, much of which relate to archaic terminology and reflect technologies that are no longer in everyday use. However, if this is not the case, and you are struggling with the concepts of opportunity cost and the time value of money, there are some excellent resources available on the Internet that can help.

Basics of Statistical Techniques

To begin analyzing data, you need only a basic understanding of statistics. To develop different modeled scenarios you can use variance and standard deviation to help provide an idea of how much of the regular daily work or activities would be captured within the innovation. For instance, 80% of all the current activity will be removed by the innovation therafter reducing the amount of time/materials/space used. These expected amounts can then be used in determining the expected savings as used in the prior section, on analytical decision-making. You will work through an example below to help demonstrate what this means and give an idea of how it might be applied in practice.

Variance

In the earlier ticket sales example a particular Zip codes spening, that gave us the average $25. Some people may have spent $30 others $20 you take all these amounts and then in another column subtract the average (mean) from each one so $30 less $25 = $5. Then take the average of all these differences of actual spending from the average spending and that is the variance.

Standard Deviation

This is the square root of the *variance*. One standard deviation is about 68% of the possible amounts of spending, so if the standard deviation was 1 that means 68% of spending was between $26 and $24, taking the $25 average plus or minus the standard deviation. Two standard deviations (literally add them together) covers 95% of potential spending amounts, and three standard deviations is 99%. So if you wanted to get an idea of the likely maximum or minimum for revenue you would add (+3 or -3) let's say that a standard deviation, in this case, was 1. That would be $1 as we were working in $ and = $3 to your $25 used, so perhaps you do a model with $28 extra per person and one with $22 extra per person.

For the bulk of the operational modeling that occurs on a daily basis, the assumption is that a distribution is normal. What this means is that when you are trying to work out how likely a particular outcome is, you can assume that the vast bulk of all the outcomes actually observed will be near the middle of any group, and symmetrically spread out towards both the highs and lows around the mean, which is what most of us think of as the average. This means that the percentage outside of the standard deviations are evenly spread for highs and lows. So if 80% were covered within your innovation there would be 10% of larger activities and 10% of the smallest activities not captured to make 100% of all the activity.

When you are looking at different resources for help with analysis, you may also come across the terms, population or sample. For most occasions, the difference between using population or sample is not going to be significant. This will change if you are using so much data that you are selecting subgroups of data to use. In this case, I would not recommend you continue unless you are very comfortable with statistics or engage someone to help you perform analysis on the information.

Using Standards for Quantitative Analysis

As you start to analyze the innovation, you may find that you need to apply a standard or come up with a process to work through. The first place you should start is by researching if there are already commonly used standards or procedures in place for quantifying a process or system, and use those. For instance, enterprise risk management deals with identifying and quantifying risk and has two widely used frameworks COSO and ISO9000. If you were in a position that you wanted to quantify the risk associated with some activities or processes that are a part of your innovation you would do well to use the methods for ranking and assessing risk that is used in one of those two standards. By leveraging existing structures, you save much duplication and can tap into the experiences of others in avoiding potential pitfalls.

If you need to put something together yourself follow some basic rules:

- Be consistent in how you apply your method.
- Keep things simple – use small numbers where posible.
- Store the data in a way that you can use – spreadsheets are not databases, but they are easy to use.
- Get data from as close to the source as possible.
- Understand what that data represents.
- Be realistic in how accurate you can be, and express that

clearly.

If you are working with data sets and information that is originating from transactions in the accounting system, then you may already have detailed information that is being quantified and treated in a standardized way. The risk here is in understanding what that data represents.

For example:

You may be interested in how much labor time the contracting process is using up. Fortunately, the whole system is based on e-signatures, so every activity about every contract is stored in the system. In this case, you probably have more data than you know what to do with, and the real issue is in making sure the data you choose accurately reflects what it is you are testing for.

For example:

You want to know how many invoices are being manually entered into a system. It is likely that there is a flag or code given to every manually entered invoice that differentiates them from system generated entries or manual entries. However, when you talk to the system administrators, you may also discover that the system creates a second record to record it in another database. If you ask simply for a count of all manual invoices it could be overstated by a factor of 2, assuming this code is left on. So when dealing with data, work closely with the system administrators to understand how it handles a transaction while thinking about what the information is to be used for. For instance, if you are looking for percentage increases from year to year, the duplication would be irrelevant, as both would increase at the same rate.However, if looking at counts to determine time spent on entering invoices, it would be very significant.

For large-scale data and analytics, it may be necessary to involve outside help in integrating various data sources and being able to extract the information you require. Always be ready to let go and bring in an expert.

Technological tools and approaches

Technological tools represent one of the most potent categories, and also one of the most complex. Technology has and continues to move at an astounding rate. Presently the use of robots, both physical and virtual, represents a significant opportunity to increase the efficiency of every work environment. While not yet common in everyday office work, it seems likely that these could become as commonplace as the computer is today. Because technology is continually changing and has a language of its own, I would suggest working with an internal technology expert from the very earliest possible moment. If you have an idea for innovation, then it is worth making contact with your someone who is knowledgeable about your own organization's technology. In many cases, this will be the IT staff. Have an informal discussion to learn how technology is implemented and managed before doing anything else; this will also give you an opportunity to find out who is the expert on the area you are interested in and what technology may already be deployed or under development that might be of use.

For the most part smaller-scale innovations, even with significant impacts, are going to be utilizing computer technology, and within that, mostly technology relating to software or personal computing devices. Broader scale hardware changes tend to be much more significant decisions that have to go through a well-established process, and so is not the focus of this book. However, that should not put off the budding innovator. If you have an idea for something bigger - find out what the process is and take the steps towards getting involved in the process.

Generally, there are a wide range of software applications that can be used to make things faster and more straightforward; most will have been tried and tested. These range in scale and options from large-scale systems that are enterprise-wide to smaller single-user software for specific uses. Be careful to ensure that, whatever the size and scope of the technical solution, the way the software can be used in standard conditions meet your needs. In general, if you are required to make substantial modifications to get it to work for you it is not the right solution. You should also be aware that the sales teams of software and solutions companies are often a headache to the technology teams by making promises of usability that are extremely difficult for the engineers who will implement any system. If you can, ask for a technical person to be present, or have your expert available to ask complex implementation and usability questions.

A beautiful use of IT is for processes and workflows, taking a manual system and automating it, adding a layer of control or increasing its accessibility. Web-based solutions are usually a cheap and easy way of getting started and in many cases may already be available to you. You may not have thought about using them for other tasks, like Google docs or even the website.

Communications can be greatly improved with the use of technology. Simple things such as using group emails that always go to a select number of people but uses a single address such as emailus@organization.org, collaborative remote workspaces and fixed processes setting up workflows so that everyone who needs to know is notified on time and if necessary has an opportunity to respond.

A common failure point for many uses of technology is the failure to leverage the efficiencies and value in the technology by attempting to simply recreate the existing processes using the technology; generally this creates additional work. An excellent example of this is implementing data analytic tools that can provide data reports from the various sources when they are replacing somewhat manual processes such as: using a spreadsheet to compile data from multiple sources, grouping, and giving specific results. Often the implementation team are dependent on the existing users to define the requirements. If the existing users do not understand what the implications or the capabilities of the tool are, and insist on specific outputs, you end up with a very sophisticated tool doing nothing more than providing the same information the spreadsheet does and still requiring the same amount of work from the users, if not more. The failure of users to understand or be willing to consider new ways of working can lead to the implementation of multiple software and technology solutions that could all be done by one; this is a very costly fault of leadership.

Sociological Tools and Approaches

The Sociological section has been subdivided into three main components to help you focus on potential tools and methods: organizational culture, building teams and, strengthening communications.

Sociological factors are the hardest to quantify, the most likely to prevent innovation and they are also the most difficult to manage. The best approach you can take is to be methodical and aware of how your own emotions and feelings, as well as experiences and background, will impact how you interpret any given situation. Some of the most catastrophic failures of change and innovation are due to not enough time and objectivity being given to review the sociological factors, and their integration into the design and implementation plan to ensure it fits the organization and individuals involved.

Organizational Culture

It is critical to have a firm understanding of the organization's culture as a whole, the culture of smaller working units within the organization and the culture that exists between the smaller working units themselves and the organization. Your knowledge and understanding of the individual working units will be a significant constraint in determining the scale of innovation you can successfully implement and should be a factor in ranking, which changes how to proceed.

In practical terms, this means getting to know how different individuals and groups are going to respond to different situations. You will need to assess individuals' levels of comfort with technology, how processes and procedures are defined and adhered to, how prevalent are informal processes and bespoke responses to situations.

The organization's culture as a whole is probably the easiest to determine as it is going to be evidenced in traits, beliefs, and attitudes that show up across workgroups and are prevalent throughout the organization. Please take note of what those commonalities are as they will be important in making sure any plan does not get caught up on a cultural snag. For many organizations, the culture is primarily driven by the senior leadership, so when possible look at how the VP and Dean level individuals interact with one another and with other employees. Keep a careful eye on how other employees respond to the senior leadership team. Are communications direct and positive, or do people do their best to go around or even exclude the senior team altogether? It takes time to determine this, but even if you do not interact directly, you can get a good idea of the culture from others who do. Understanding how senior leadership organizes and communicates will help you to identify the type of innovation that is most likely to be successful and receive support from the senior leadership.

When assessing the organization's culture, be careful to make assessments using as much information as possible and over time. An organization is formed of people, organizing together to achieve common objectives and goals. People can give various impressions depending on the day, relationships, and time of year.

People are also influenced and likely to make decisions on past experiences. If you are new to an organization you will not have the institutional awareness of what events and experiences those around you have had within the organization in the recent past that might negatively impact on an initiative. Perhaps something very similar was tried but not handled well and left many convinced it is not possible. In some cases individuals that are generally helpful and supportive, but have been with an organization for some years, may not think of historical events that could cause issues. Because of this blind spot for everyday tasks it is essential when you engage long-term partners to ask them about past initiatives or implementations directly and talk through recent historical events within the organization that connects to any initiative you may be hoping to implement.

Building Teams

Building teams is closely linked to strengthening communications below, and to the culture above. It is also about learning how to organize well together, finding out what the strengths of the individuals are and building enough trust that when things go wrong, the result is learning rather than blame.

There is a vast amount of research and many texts on how to build teams that you can read to fully develop those skills. To get things going and to give you an idea of some practical approaches that have worked well for me, and which are relatively easy to implement with a bit of work on your side, consider these:

- Information or educational events like lunch and learns. You just need to pick something you know about and would like to share, book a meeting room and invite others to come. You can try to make it a regular occurrence and solicit others to present. My tip would be to make these regular but no more than monthly.

- Bakeoffs (or other food-based events). These need a bit more organizing and requires people who like to cook. You could easily adapt it to some other shared culinary interest.

- Potlucks are an easy way to get lunch for a group together on a low budget and to organize and a fun way for everyone to get together for a shared experience.

- Office games. This will depend on the organization but depending on what it's like you could consider: competitions such as trivia, or card games such as Uno or for the more adventurous games such as statues.

- Outings to group events like bowling. These are classic team events, and for a reason. You get out onto neutral ground and have an opportunity to talk about something other than work. If you are in a big enough organization, you may be able to get funding to help cover some of the costs.

Setting up fun work time events that bring people together helps to build a comfortable working relationship that can be endlessly useful. By allowing people to chat and get to know one another, you can tackle some of the most significant issues faced while implementing change, such as simply not knowing whom to talk to. Having trust in one another can also help generate new ideas and improve collaboration overall. Events could be anything you enjoy and that you think others in the organization would be interested in.

You may find you need to organize a couple of different events as not everyone will want to do all the activities. You must be careful not to exclude others inadvertently, and in doing so create a bubble of individuals around you who just think and act like you. Ultimately this means you will need to go to some events that are not as appealing to you as well.

Strengthening Communications

Communication is a lot more complicated and requires more thought than we generally give time too. Email, for instance, provides a false sense of security in the knowledge of what is being communicated. Emails are in general short through necessity and environment, such as being written on a telephone on the train for instance, lack the precision which might be applied to other written communications. That, coupled with the lack of additional information such as tone of voice, facial expressions, and body language can leave the bulk of what is being communicated unsent. Emoticons, I do not believe, quite bridge that gap and risk ironic or sarcastic interpretation ☺. I am not opposed to email, but I am in support of considering what communication medium to use and how. Taking the time to think whether an email, telephone call, video conference, meeting in person, presentation or putting things onto the internet is the right medium and how much time to spend reviewing the content, will help get information sent and heard correctly.

There are numerous programs, online resources, and tools for helping to build communications between different groups and to help you identify strengths and weaknesses in your communications. As an individual, the ability to communicate is critical if you want to get things done. Consider not just involve getting your point across, but to listen and understand what it is that others are saying. Listening is generally the most challenging area to tackle, and the most important. It is the most difficult because you really cannot make someone change how he or she listens. You can, however, learn how they listen and, in the short term, adapt the way you send information to be heard.

Below are three practical steps in which you can adapt information being sent to strengthen communications.

1. Firstly identify times when you have noticed the person with whom you wish to communicate take on and truly understand what was being communicated. How did that happen?

   What was the medium, email, face to face or something else?

   What information was included. Were there lots of pleasantries or was it straightforward?

   What type of language was used, very simple short words or highly complex elucidating promulgations?

Where was this information passed, in a formal meeting, in a group email or one to one, and who was involved?

2. Once you have identified how the person best listens then try to adapt the information to be ideally suited to that format. If its email makes sure you are succinct with the information you have to share, make the email easily readable with lots of space and bullets. If it's a telephone call make sure they have time to talk and are not doing something else, which applies to face to face too.

3. As a rule of thumb - Say hello, how are you, thank you and be direct. In my experience, most people appreciate being treated as intelligent human beings, whose availability is limited, but still, have enough of it to share some pleasantries and connect as individuals.

There are many ways to communicate and determining the optimum tool is not always obvious. Below is a communication tools matrix as a place to start. This matrix is based on the most common scenario of a group working in an office or local offices. You may find that the orders of the chart need to be adapted for larger groups, or those spread over a larger geographical area.

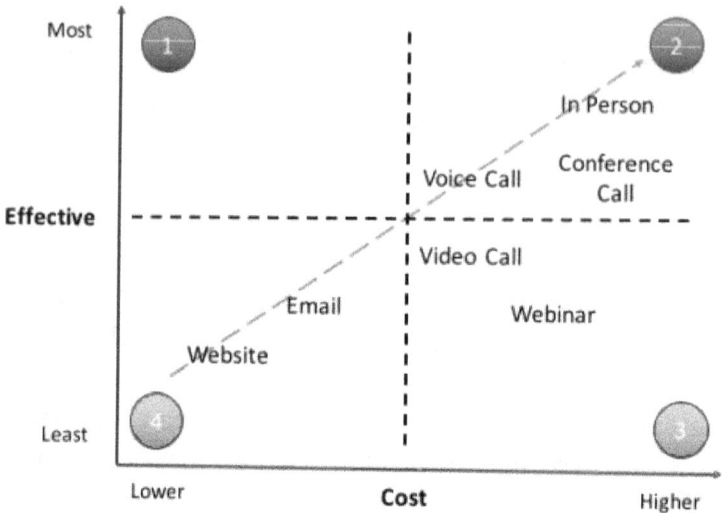

These are some of the common ways we communicate. The most significant driver of costs here is people and their time. The purple dotted line, from zone four to zone two illustrates the standard flow of communications as the information becomes increasingly important. We will soon take a look at some best practices and uses of the four tools this purple line runs through.

The other tools all have excellent uses and can be employed in very practical ways, especially if dealing with a geographically dispersed group. One item you may wonder about is the ranking of voice call verses video call; honestly, I don't think video calls are as useful just because it is not quite in person and not quite distant. Often having to attempt to make eye contact with the screen, where the camera is set above the face, feels uncomfortable. Trying to maintain eye contact can become a distraction to the conversation. Video calls also tend to have the issues of conference calls where background noises get picked up. When there is background noise it becomes hard to tell when a sentence is complete, and the speaker has finished; it can be difficult for others to tell when someone else is getting ready to talk, so people tend to run over each other. This can trend towards stifling conversation.

As mentioned before this chart is for the most commonly occurring situations. Some circumstances might alter the cost or effectiveness of a form of communication so you should be evaluating how vital it is for the message to be communicated and is that cost to benefit ratio right for you.

IMPLEMENTATION OF THE PLAN

After all of the careful planning and preparation work is done, you are ready to begin. Arguably you already have been implementing your innovation since you first thought of it and decided to move forward through the activities described in previous chapters. Once you start executing the detailed plan you are setting off a chain of events that will commit significant resources, including your own time, to getting the initiative successfully implemented. You are also committing yourself to completing the project.

DEVELOPING RELATIONSHIPS AND BUILDING TRUST

As you develop tools and an understanding of the organization, you will very likely have some other tasks to do in order to carry on with your regular work. It is through your regular activities that you can start to build a strong foundation that will ultimately enable you to implement innovation. However, to be effective, you must have built up trust in your competence and abilities, not only with leaders but also with your peers and co-workers. To build trust, you must develop a reputation as someone who is competent and has excellent awareness of the areas of the three necessary tools from the previous sub-section. To help speed this process along there are several things you can do.

Firstly, be mindful of your normal assigned responsibilities, make sure that your regular job is being done well. Your first projects should be in making sure your activities, and working practices are optimal. Look at what innovations and changes can you implement. Not only can this help give you more time to dedicate to other projects, it is a beautiful opportunity to practice. If it does not work out, chances are the only person who is negatively impacted is you. Moreover, if you're going to make mistakes, learning by doing, then make mistakes on a small scale with limited.

Be willing to take on and work on all projects as they arrive, regardless of if they forward your own personal projects or beliefs in what needs to be done. Take every opportunity to be a member of a team, and once you have been a team member on some projects, start offering to take a leadership position for parts of the next project. You can join teams in a minor role if that is more comfortable for you, starting with smaller and simpler things, such as writing up notes or collecting information. Once you have been working for a while, you will have an idea of the areas in which you excel, and you will be able, to some extent, choose to work on areas of projects that use those skills more. Building trust is a slow, incremental, and delicate process but it is also straightforward. Treat everything you do as important and offer to help.

Get your hands dirty, and when you are working with a team of people, when you see an opportunity to help out more, then do so. During a project offer support and encouragement to the rest of the team, including those on the team who may be more senior. Chances are the more senior they are, the less often people offer them encouragement. Even when you have breezed through the tasks you were assigned and volunteered for, make sure to be available to support everyone else. Especially offer support to those people who ended up with an ugly task, they may not want, or be in a position to accept help but will appreciate your offer. It is essential to remember, all that really matters is how the project does; that's all anyone else outside of your team will see, including senior leadership who ultimately will be the ones who decide if later significant innovations take place.

Being part of a successful project will also help to build excellent working relationships. When you are putting your own team together, you will already have great people to work with, who work well together and trust each other to ensure the project is a success.

Generally, when you are trying to build trust, it is better to proceed slowly and resist the urge to jump ahead. Do not take on more than you are ready for, even if offered. It is better to pass up an opportunity that you know you cannot do than to take on something and do it poorly. Being self-aware is an integral part of teamwork, and unless you know when to step back, you could cause significant problems later on. That does not mean you would not push yourself to try new things. If you don't you will never learn, but merely be realistic about your abilities and how much you can do. There is a difference between working with an expert and being the expert. If something does go horribly wrong, remember that damage to trust is not likely to be permanent. However, even small missteps and mistakes may set you back in the trust-building process, which after months or years of painstaking development is disappointing.

That risk of failure brings us into being willing to fail. Being willing to fail and at the same time able to demonstrate the ability to handle failures and overcome obstacles is an equally essential skill set to demonstrate. Sometimes things go wrong and how we deal with those failures is critical, and I would be shocked if nothing went wrong. It's the nature of a complex interconnected world. Depending on the size and scale of a failure you will need to decide what is the next best most desirable outcome, that is now feasible under the current conditions. Determining the next best outcome requires the same considerations points as the original planning - balancing those three same areas. However, you may not have the luxury of time so you should add that as part of the considerations for planning. Does the whole thing need to be postponed? Consider all the options you can think of as if you were beginning anew and what decisions you would make only from this point in time. Do not make planning decisions based solely on the fact that you have already spent money on something or invested a great deal of time on the part of the project. Those are referred to as 'sunk costs,' and they are irrelevant to future decision-making. If they don't work for the current conditions, then they don't work and should be dropped before they consume any more resources.

ENGAGING A SPONSOR

For a smaller innovation that does not involve anyone other than you, it usually will not be necessary to have a sponsor, and you would not need to include others or find funding. For larger projects engaging a sponsor is a critical part of the process and consists of bringing on-board your sponsor, a senior person who will be an advocator for you and lend you credibility so that all the other individuals you need are going to be willing to help. Your sponsor should be a person who is in a position to either authorize, or directly get authorized, the changes you need.

Ideally, your sponsor will be someone who you already have developed a strong working relationship with, and who has familiarity with the area of innovation. When designing an engagement plan, you need to think about the project from your sponsor's perspective. By thinking about and answering these three questions you can build a strong case for support.

1. Is this a valuable initiative to the organization?

2. Will other requirements and priorities still happen with this initiative taking place?

3. Do I feel comfortable that this person can implement successfully?

The first question should be answered with the data and information you have already collected and used to develop your plan. If there is a great deal of information, you should highlight the data that your sponsor is more familiar with and/or which they may perceive as primary benefits.

The second question will require you to look at the planning documents and to determine how much time and when you and others will need to be involved. You need to show how your plan is implemented without inhibiting other necessary functions; it may be that consultants or temporary staffing are required and this should be made clear up front, and as a part of the value calculations.

The third question will be demonstrated with the detailed planning and preparation work you have already done. Having a clear and well-defined path will help provide comfort. However, this will also depend on the relationship you have with the sponsor and how they perceive your current work, so it is essential not to allow other tasks to slip.

When you begin to engage the sponsor this is also the point to start talking to any individuals whom you will need to be heavily involved in the project, letting them know what you are thinking and gauging their interest, and informally asking for their input and thoughts. You can use this initial feedback to update the plan, taking into account any changes you may need to make. These early conversations will also help identify others who are excited about the idea and who will help cheerlead the project. You may find surprises in who is excited, and that may make you change your plans on whom to involve, when and how.

When you are first engaging others in the initiative, you should follow the same basic process you did for engaging the sponsor. Think about it from their perspective and listen to their ideas and opinions, and be prepared to address them all in a rational and positive way. The more you can engage others in the project, either with work or enthusiasm, the more likely it is to succeed.

If an initiative will impact the day-to-day activities of a group of people, it is even more important to make sure they feel some ownership and have an opportunity to voice concerns and make suggestions. Go through the detailed plan, or section that is relevant to a group or individual. Walk through how you came up with the initial draft, and what you are thinking and planning. Give them a chance to find flaws and identify issues so they can be addressed long before you are committed to a specific path, and be willing to accept suggestions for improvements. Think about any suggested improvements and be careful not to fall into the trap of seeing the plan as a fixed document that dictates what will happen. Rather it is a map, which needs to be updated as new information arrives.

Depending on the organization's culture, you may have different options for working with other individuals and reviewing the plan. In all cases, make sure to identify a single decision maker for each specific issue, or point of discussion and communicate this to everyone involved. If there are a limited set of options available, make sure to clearly state these before, during and at the end of a discussion so that the group does not feel like they were unheard. If there is a significant issue that is brought up be willing to take it away and research it further. You may decide that the project can continue in a slightly different form and add this concern to the project plan as a second stage so that the entire initiative is not derailed.

When engaging others, refer to the communications plan you developed, use those same basic frameworks for communication, look at the people you needed involved and make sure you have begun to engage them in some way. Prepare to adapt the communication plan to the actual realities you are seeing that are different to your initial assumptions.

DETAILED IMPLEMENTATION STEPS

The first step to implementing your plan is to do a final check of the individuals and resources you need to be involved. Check-in and confirm time frames and availabilities as well as confirm with them your expectations of tier involvement in detail. This is the time to find out if you need to make a substitution or include someone else. If, during this stage, you find you need to make a substitution or another substantial change, be willing to assess the impact and accept you may have to wait and miss any original windows rather than try to rush through and risk failure due to shoddy work or errors.

Who - Look through the plan and identify all the individuals involved. Make sure to prioritize the people involved earliest and those who are critical, because they are hard to replace or the task is complex.

How – Review the communications part of your plan. Have you already identified any particular processes to make communicating easier? If you have identified processes, use this time as an opportunity to test run and refine them.

The second step is to arrange any meetings and start to start work; this includes handing out any work that needs to be completed by others. If you are using a third party consultant make sure you ask for mockups or samples of what they will be producing and set specific time frames to review so you can confirm that what they are producing is what you want.

Start at the beginning of the detailed plan by requesting or confirming tasks to be performed. Where tasks can be run concurrently make sure to do as many as you feel you can manage, without losing sight and control of what is being produced. If there are many concurrent tasks that are absolutely necessary, make sure to delegate responsibility to others and regularly check in with one another to stay on track.

Be specific and methodical in starting work. Give clear and straightforward instructions and confirm requirements from others. Keep track of the work that is being handed out or undertaken, including your own, and make sure to affirm due dates and set up check-in times. Even if you have already communicated a set of time frames, make sure that you confirm individually and get a positive response. Early on get into the habit of testing that what you are developing is in line with what you expected and that the assumptions you have made are holding true.

From now on, you are following your detailed plan. Keeping track of tasks being performed by others either through regular meetings, emails or other communications. As you find the need to make changes update the detailed plan, and review what potential these changes have to impact on other parts of the plan. Whatever communications method you are using make sure to check on any "products" (either physical items, data or the result of any work being undertaken) that they are in line with what you need. Checking on products, or outputs will help ensure you don't waste anyone's time through the need to rework.

CRISIS MANAGEMENT

Earlier in the planning section we touched on the necessity to include a crisis management outline to any planning in order to be prepared for the possibility of something going wrong. While there may be significant events that appear as a crisis, things have not gone horribly wrong until you fail to manage them. The nature of the crisis and the cultural environment you work in will have an essential part in how these things play out. When you are working on a project, something will go wrong. It could be big or small, but if it involves other people, you will be faced with containing a situation before it gets out of hand. If you are in a culture of reactivism, how you respond is going to be even more important.

Reactivism can be loosely defined as: *"basing decisions on how you feel and acting on them - before you have all of the facts."* It is a trait contained in many organizational cultures and is a source of enormous instability and waste. Please do not succumb to it.

Of all the things you can do the most important is to STOP just for a few seconds, be calm, focus, and be present. Then, Examine, Plan and Execute. Follow the general steps from above, balancing the three areas but also identifying how to stabilize each one. Prevent further damage and give yourself time to prioritize. Think about which factors are going to cause the most damage and come up with a plan to improve those first. A typical example of this is within the Sociological factor. Communicate what has happened and let those directly impacted or already aware know what activity is going on to correct it. Even if the only information you have to give is that "...you are aware of the issue and working on different solutions." This action can help stop the spread of misinformation. It identifies whom concerned individuals should speak with (you or a trusted team member) and helps reduce anxiety for others, as they do not have to worry about being responsible for a situation.

Now be cautious here when communicating, "letting those directly impacted or already aware know." Directly impacted is a tricky bit. It sounds concrete but it is not. By "directly" I generally mean:

> Those individuals or groups whom you will **need to talk to**, or give details to, in order to get a situation corrected, and/or are going to **be impacted** by the error **before** it can be corrected.

Now the issue may have the potential to impact any number of people, but if they are not going to be impacted before it is fixed, do not involve them during the crisis management phase. The rule of thumb is to keep the communications small and controlled. You may later decide that a wider discussion needs to take place. Perhaps the fix requires some changes and you want input from the wider community. If so, that should be part of a well-managed communications plan where you are aware of all the facts and options available and can offer a guided discussion.

Please also be extremely careful of any fast-talking and loud voices that appear in any situation, especially when there is some 'crisis' occurring. If you are the loud, fast talker, think about what you are trying to achieve and follow the advice from before. Stop! Fast-talking is generally a substitute for careful thought. Talking quickly and loudly may have been found by the talker to be an excellent way of getting things done and making things happen, especially in ossified environments. Loud, fast, talking does one job very well though, and that is to be distracting, and make thinking clearly more difficult for others. When in a crisis agree to nothing and request a moment to consider, especially if you are required to make a decision on the fly. Many of the best decision makers I have worked with have been extraordinarily soft-spoken but firm in their requirement to have the time to think about what decisions they wanted to make.

ADDING ADDITIONAL VALUE

You can add additional value and help to steady the process by getting into the habit of regularly reviewing the plan and comparing and contrasting it to the reality you are experiencing. Executing the plan will require you to continually reflect where everything is in relation to the detailed plan, as well as what is going on in the organization as a whole. It also requires you to manage the process by following up with individuals and reviewing the outcomes of communications. If you have teams working on any particular piece of the project, you will need to manage those teams by making sure the team is functioning optimally. Before you put the team together, make sure you are aware of the strengths and weaknesses of each member by getting to know them. During the project periodically verify that the skills of the individuals involved are being used appropriately. Check that you give the team clear goals and guidelines for how you expect them to interact as a team and with others involved. Provide them with the authority necessary to make decisions without holding up the project and clearly define the authorization processes and limitations.

You will also need to try and identify potential issues or opportunities in advance. Where you identify potential problems, or areas of uncertainty, that are critical to a successful implementation, you will need to create detailed backup plans that allow you to continue depending on what you think the two or three most likely outcomes are from any uncertain situation.

For example: As part of your plan, you are relying on adaptations to a software tool. Past adaptations to this software tool have not gone well, and you want to make sure the project stays on track. So you come up with the ideal Plan A, which is what you would like to happen, but it requires many modifications to the tool. You also develop a Plan B that involves a minimum of modifications of the tool. It is not as ideal as Plan A, but it is functional and likely to be completed well within the time frame. Depending on the overall planning process and how important the software tool is, you may be able to switch to B if A encounters issues or you may need to concurrently develop A and B together so that if A fails B is already in place.

SUSTAINING THE MOMENTUM

An essential part of executing the plan is in keeping the momentum of the project going, which requires keeping up motivation for yourself and others.

1. Sponsor - You should keep your sponsor involved and positively engaged in what is happening, don't just go to them with issues or requests but also periodically report or present on important milestones reached, or particularly tricky obstacles overcome, and keep reminding them of why it is crucial and exciting and why they supported you in the beginning.

2. Peers and staff – Be a cheerleader for every single person working with you. Point out their successes and be free with your praise of hard work and successful completion of goals. Consistently remind everyone of how the work they are doing is going to produce an essential and exciting innovation.

3. Yourself – Be consistent and methodical in how you work to help stave off any fears of making errors, and to be absolutely confident in what you are doing. Being methodical will help you to stay calm and focused when dealing with naysayers and those who are nervous

about the impact of any changes and prevent you from becoming disillusioned or disheartened.

4. Everyone – Have fun and make sure you take all the opportunities to enjoy the process whenever you can. Support others during the tougher moments and be open to support yourself.

Keeping the momentum of a change going also requires being willing to weigh the time to loss of adjusting to unexpected constraints. That may mean you cannot achieve everything you had hoped. Be prepared to make tough decisions and to think carefully about the value of an innovation. Consider, "Is the constraint a requirement, or would it be better to continue forward with 80% of the original value being realized?"

SUMMARY

Executing is a constant cycle that begins with the implementation of the existing plan, and then, revisions to the plan for actual experiences encountered. This cycle of implementing and revising will constantly happen until the project is completed. Your objective is to manage this cycle and keep it running smoothly by caring for the tasks that keep it rolling, and by removing obstacles in its path.

LEARNING FROM YOUR INNOVATION

As you work through the implementation of every innovation, you gain insight into what has worked well and what has worked less well, what you would do differently and what you would do again. Often what works or does not work is dependent on the specific innovation you are working on and the environment you are working in. However, general lessons and knowledge can be gained by reviewing every implementation. Reflecting on prior implementations and changes gives you invaluable insight into your own organization and is a fantastic opportunity for you to develop your expertise. By being organized and methodical, you can maximize how much you learn and grow and get the most value out of every experience.

EVALUATE

Once your project is completed, you have one last very important thing to do: reflect on the entire process, review your notes, compare the initial plan to the final results and put down in writing the things that went well and the things that did not.

Once you have a list of good and bad it is time to analyze each one and determine the root cause of the success or failure; this may involve thinking back a few steps along the path to each one to find the origin point.

For example

Part of the innovation involved a web interface that was coded by in-house developers, however it was designed to be displayed properly only in Internet Explorer (IE), but there is a fifth of the users that use Chrome and for whom it was unreadable. The developers fixed it, but it added time and cost. What was the error? Well making it only readable in IE is the first answer, certainly for the users, but that was the result of a decision made early on in the process to minimize the use of the developer's time and keep costs down by only coding it to one web browser. The decision to use only one web browser, in turn, was based on the assumption that everyone could use IE. Why did we think everyone could use IE? That information was based on the result of the questions in the initial user requirements questionnaires, which were used to set the specifications. How was the user survey defined? We came up with questions ourselves. Moreover, here is the origination point, and this is the first opportunity where another decision being made could have prevented the fix being required.

Reviewing this example, we can list out what we have learned for the future:

1. Next time circulating the list of user requirement questions with the technical team, and possibly others may be a great way of preventing this type of error in the future (Although it's not guaranteed, it should reduce the likelihood).

2. That whenever we are asking questions of others on behalf of others, we need to make sure we get all the details. Ensuring comprehensive details are collected could be thought of as an ordering problem; we asked questions to set requirements before we knew all the parameters that would be needed.

3. Never assume the technical team will catch your mistakes, they are going to believe that if you ask them for something, it's exactly what you want.

As you can see from this one problem, we have learned several different things. Keep in mind this is a positive, learning, and skill building experience. As such, this is not supposed to be a process of finding villains or apportioning blame. The purpose is to help build up your knowledge through each experience and learn. Every project is going to be different and present new problems, but by learning from the past and applying that to the future, you can very quickly learn to identify potential future hazards and prevent them before they occur. It is also essential to understand the origins of why things went well too, which is generally even more fun, especially when you discover that the root cause of some of the success turned out to be blind luck. If you're like me, you may find those the most exciting.

Even if there is a formal 'lessons learned' or another debrief afterward, do this simple process independently, just for yourself. Use the official process and if necessary, build it out to meet your own needs. In general, I have not often seen an official debrief that was more than an exercise to either apportion blame for a failed project or ended up as another hassle with people just going through the motions. Even if this is the case, use the opportunity to your advantage, and encourage others to do the same. If you are going to go through a process and spend your time on something, then make sure you get the best value out of it you possibly can!

To summarize: understanding how you work and where your strengths and weaknesses are. It will help you to be more effective and focus your attention to strengthening weaknesses and pulling in resources to bolster them while being able to reduce the resourcesin areas where you are strong enough to carry on without them.

SOME THINGS TO HELP

H ere are a few descriptions of practical day to day tools for planning and keeping track of information.

Excel Gant Template

Gant charts are excellent tools to use in working out the sequencing of events and helping to identify time-based constraints. They are an excellent first step to thinking about all the various steps involved and putting them together over time. This as a process is a great way to help break up planning into smaller more manageable pieces to fill in the details and work out what materials might be needed.

Basic Word Memo

Having a standard format for communicating and documenting the project will help everyone easily identify where to look for guidance and help to create a feeling of substance to your implementation. This, in turn, can help to keep a plan moving along by generating momentum. The standard formatting should be in line with your organization's standards for colors and fonts as well as be adapted to make it clear that it relates to the project for your innovation. This can be used to communicate more official information, to establish meeting agendas, write out simple instructions or guides, or even to keep a list of action items you want to track.

Basic PowerPoint Presentation

PowerPoint slides are not just for stand-up presentations they can be used to help tell any story; this may be training material for using technology, or even understanding the steps of a process or project. When using PowerPoint, try to keep the amount of information on any one slide to a minimum and the number of slides below twenty. Integrate graphics and words as evenly as possible and if it does not fit on one slide without being very small or hard to look at, break it down into pieces.

Also, as with the Word document, and in all the other materials around your project, create a template with the colors and fonts already set so it can be quickly and easily used. You can do this by editing the Slide Master. Changes made to the slides in the slide master view will appear on all the slides used in the regular view, depending on which type of slide you edit in the Slide Master and changing colors and fonts for each of the different master slides.

You Can Make A Difference

You can be the innovator inside your organization by letting out the innovator inside you!

www.ingramcontent.com/pod-product-compliance
Lightning Source LLC
Chambersburg PA
CBHW070425240526
45472CB00020B/1298